THE OFFICIAL
ENGLAND
RUGBY

ANNUAL 2011

ENGLAND RUGBY

Written by Martin Johnston

A Grange Publication

© 2010. Published by Grange Communications Ltd., Edinburgh, under licence from the RFU. © 2009 Rugby Football Union. The England Rose is an official trade mark of the Rugby Football Union and is the subject of extensive trade mark registration worldwide. Printed in the EU.

Photographs © RFU and Press Association Images

ISBN 978-1-907104-80-0

£7.99

CONTENTS

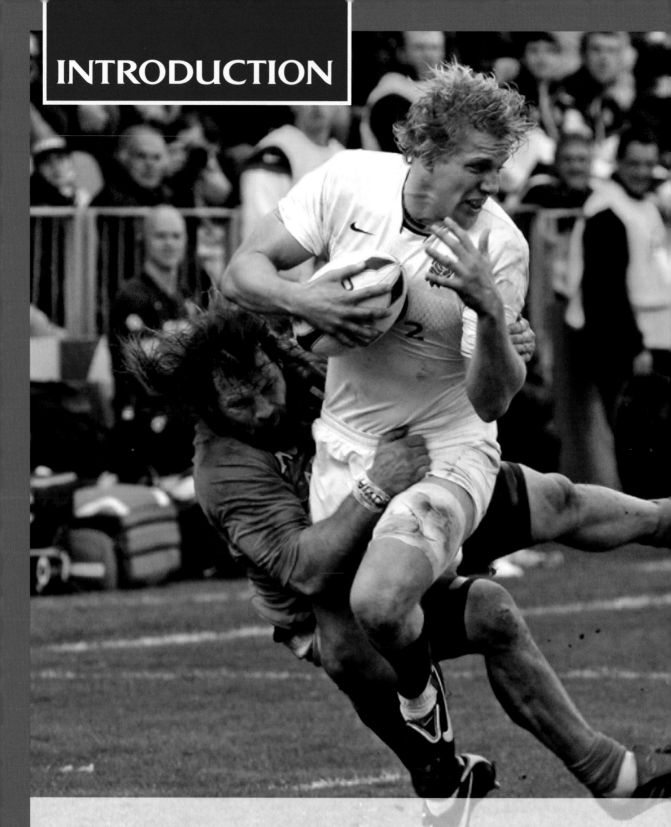

INTRODUCTION

Welcome to The Official England Rugby Annual 2011. We've got another fantastic collection of articles and pictures for you for this year.

As England prepare for the Rugby World Cup 2011 in New Zealand, we take a look at the tournament and see how the squad is preparing. We also check in with the players in the senior team and run the rule over some more potential stars of the future.

As usual, there are also stacks of exclusive features on all the other important stuff like

England Saxons, England Sevens and the other England representative sides.

As well as features on the key players, we also find out a few more details behind the stats. Which player had soccer trials for Liverpool and who nearly signed for Arsenal? Who started their career at one of the smaller clubs like Otley or Northampton Old Scouts? Find out inside.

There's lots of fun stuff too, like The Big England Quiz, a spot the ball, a rugby wordsearch and a crossword. Enjoy!

England: Rugby World Cup 2011 Progress Report

England head to the Rugby World Cup in New Zealand in 2011 with a great pedigree in the competition, but how is the current squad shaping up?

After playing host to the very first Rugby World Cup in 1987, New Zealand will have the honour again in 2011 and will be very hard to beat on home soil.

For the 2011 tournament 20 teams will play in four pools of five each. England play in Pool B, as second seeds behind Argentina.

It's a bit of a cliché in the world of sport, but there are definitely no easy games at a World Cup tournament. England will be keen to put in some good performances and progress through the tournament.

England's first game is against Argentina in Christchurch, where they also play Georgia. But will they be ready? The answer is probably "Yes" – especially if they can add some discipline in defence and clinical finishing to their traditionally powerful forward play.

The intensity of the games in the tour down under in 2010 showed that they are certainly tough enough to take on any pack in the world and with more consistency in the line-out will be as good as any team in the competition.

England at the RWC 2011 – Four Players to Watch:

CHRIS ASHTON
Chris Ashton's try-scoring abilities can't be questioned. A deadly finisher who's background in rugby league also made him a tough tackler. Odds-on to be England's top try scorer.

COURTNEY LAWES
Youth is definitely on Courtney Lawes' side, which probably accounts for his mobility and speed in open play. Great assets for a lock! He has come a long way in a short time. In 2009 he was playing for England Under 20s at the IRB Junior World Cup in Japan.

TOBY FLOOD
Toby Flood has already amassed 31 caps, starting for England 18 times. His versatility is one of the reasons he is so invaluable to the team, having played regularly at both fly half and centre. He is more than likely to be a key player in this World Cup Squad.

DYLAN HARTLEY
New Zealand-born Dylan Hartley will relish the chance to show the country of his birth his true value on the field. Likely to be first choice at hooker, Dylan is a combative, all-action player who loves to get the ball in his hands and take the game to the opposition.

RBS 6 Nations 2010 Round Up

The 2010 RBS 6 Nations was a roller coaster ride for England and their fans. Martin Johnson's men started well, stalled in the middle and ended on a high, despite losing an extraordinary final game in Paris. A game which left France as deserved, if surprisingly unadventurous, Grand Slam winners.

WEEKEND ONE

With England celebrating Twickenham's centenary by wearing unbranded retro-style shirts specially designed by Nike, a first-day win was really important. Steve Borthwick's men duly delivered; winning 30-17 with James Haskell grabbing two tries despite the almost inevitable Welsh fight back. In Dublin, Ireland stumbled past Italy 29-11, while France edged out a competitive Scots side 9-18 at Murrayfield.

WEEKEND TWO

England were unconvincing 17-12 victors in Rome and could only conjure up one try against a feisty Italy. Matthew Tait scored

the only try of the game, while Jonny Wilkinson joined Ronan O'Gara in the 6 Nations 500-point club. In Cardiff, Scotland seemed on course for their first win in Wales since 2002 until a last-gasp Shane Williams try gave the home side a 31-24 win. In Paris, France laid down a marker for their Grand Slam intentions, easily beating Ireland 33-10.

WEEKEND THREE

It was Tommy Bowe's day at Twickenham as he scored a try at the start and end of Ireland's 16-20 win. Dan Cole became the first prop to score for England since 2006 and Jonny Wilkinson kicked 11 points. But Keith Earls added a try to Bowe's brace and O'Gara's boot did the rest. In Paris, France and Wales scored two tries each but Morgan Parra's kicking was the difference in a 26-20 win. At the Stadio Flaminio, Pablo Canavosio's try gave Italy a 16-12 win over Scotland.

WEEKEND FOUR

A dour, try-less encounter dominated by kicking saw England retain the Calcutta Cup at Murrayfield. They could only draw the game 15-15, however, as Scotland's Dan Parks scored a drop goal and four penalties to England's five penalties. Jonny Wilkinson chalked up three and Toby Flood two. France moved a step closer to the Grand Slam beating Italy 46-20, scoring six tries. In Dublin, Tomas O'Leary inspired a back-on-track Ireland to a 27-12 win over Wales.

WEEKEND FIVE

England confounded their critics in the final game in Paris, showing an attacking mentality that should have yielded more than the 10 points they ended the game with. Ben Foden scored the game's only try but an uncharacteristically defensive French performance saw them grind out the 12-10 win they so desperately needed to clinch the Grand Slam. At Croke Park, Scotland denied Ireland the Triple Crown with a shock 23-20 last-gasp win, while James Hook scored two tries in Wales' 33-10 victory over Italy.

FINAL TABLE

	W	D	L	T	F	A	Pts
1. France	5	0	0	13	135	69	10
2. Ireland	3	0	2	11	106	95	6
3. England	2	1	2	6	88	76	5
4. Wales	2	0	3	10	113	117	4
5. Scotland	1	1	3	3	83	100	3
6. Italy	1	0	4	5	69	137	2

Ben Foden

In 2010 Ben Foden fulfilled all the promise of his 2009 PRA Young Player of the Year Award with a great season for Northampton Saints and a scintillating try on his full England debut in Paris.

Chester-born Ben Foden made his England debut in the 2009 RBS 6 Nations as a replacement against Italy. He went on to make his full debut in Paris in the final game of the 2010 tournament. With only six minutes on the clock Foden showed what he is capable of in full flow. He then kept his place as first choice full back for Martin Johnson in the next two tests against Australia.

He earned his call-up on the back of some outstanding displays at both scrum half and full back for Northampton. He joined the Saints in summer 2008 after spending four years at Sale Sharks, where he had graduated from the Sale academy Jets squad. At Franklin's Gardens he linked up again with his former England U21s coach Jim Mallinder, who gave him the opportunity to play in both positions.

Ben was a member of the 2006 Grand Slam-winning England U21s squad, playing in all five matches and scoring three tries. He also scored a try on his debut for England Saxons in 2009 and won the PRA's Young Player of the Year Award in the same year.

CLUB:	Northampton Saints
POSITION:	Scrum half/Full back
BORN:	22.07.1985 I Chester
HEIGHT:	1.83m (6' 0")
WEIGHT:	94kg (14st 12lb)
REPRESENTATIVE HONOURS:	Cheshire & North of England U16s, England A U16s, England U19s, England Counties, England U21s (2005 6 Nations v W, F, I, It, S) World Championships v W, It, S, F, I , 2006 6 Nations and World Championships, England Sevens (2006/07 Dub, George, Well, San D, Adelaide, 2007/08 Dub, George), England Saxons (2008 Barclays Churchill Cup v USA, I(R), S(R))
CAPS:	6
POINTS:	5 – 1T
INTERNATIONAL RECORD:	2009 It(R), 2010 F, I(R), S(R), A (1, 2)

13

DID YOU KNOW?
Ben loves to exercise his vocal chords and his nickname is 'Pop Idol' because, when he was 18, he entered the TV show of that name. He had been a singer in a band called Anonymous when he was 13.

Ben's dad Rob, who currently coaches Chester RFC, was a big influence on his career.

Spot the Difference

Look at the two pictures below. Can you spot six differences between them?

ANSWERS ON PAGE 60

The Big England Rugby Quiz

1. Which two teams played in the Guinness Premiership Grand Final in 2010?

2. Ben Foden made his debut for England at full back. What other position can he play?

3. Who is England's *second* highest ever points scorer in the 6 Nations tournament?

4. A cockerel features on the badge of which of England's RBS 6 Nations rivals?

5. What colour are England's away shirts?

6. England's biggest ever win was 134-0 against Japan. True or false?

7. Who captained England in their annual match against the Barbarians in 2010?

8. Which famous international sevens tournament did England win for three years in a row, 2004-2006?

9. For which premiership club does England Sevens and Under 20s flyer, Christian Wade play?

10. Who is the official patron of the RFU?

11. For which French club does James Haskell play?

12. What is the surname of England squad siblings Delon and Steffon?

13. England EPS squad member Hendre Fourie was born in which country?

14. In which annual transatlantic tournament do England Saxons currently compete?

15. Which team won the 2010 LV= Cup Final?

16. What is the current capacity of Twickenham Stadium?

17. England's first ever full-time coach was Don White, appointed in 1969. True or false?

18. Which experienced hooker was a late replacement for the injured Dylan Hartley in England's 2010 summer tour squad?

19. Which England assistant coach played 398 times as a prop for Leicester Tigers?

20. What is the official name of the Rugby World Cup trophy?

ANSWERS ON PAGE 60

A WHOLE NEW Ball Game

JSC
England Rugby Junior Supporters Club

There's a NEW England Rugby Junior Supporters Club coming soon. September's the month to look out for an exciting new club for all young England Rugby fans.

If you want more information or might want to join email hopeandglory@rfu.com

NEW JUNIOR SUPPORTERS CLUB LAUNCHING SOON!

England v France: Le Crunch in the Rugby World Cup

One of the most eagerly anticipated international fixtures of any season, England v France matches have always had a special atmosphere. So much so that they have gained their own nickname, *'Le Crunch'*. Here we look at the Rugby World Cup matches played between the two sides.

The very first game between the two countries was on March 22, 1906 at the Parc des Princes, in Paris. England won that game 8-35. The first ever Rugby World Cup meeting between the sides was at the same venue in 1991, which England also won 10-19.

France then gained revenge by winning the 3rd/4th play-off game of the 1995 Rugby World Cup, 19-9 in Pretoria, South Africa.

England have also played France in two of the most recent Rugby World Cup semi-finals, winning on both occasions. In 2003 in the Telstra Dome in Sydney, Australia, Jonny Wilkinson scored a hat-trick of goals to help England secure a 24-7 win and a place in the final against the hosts.

In 2007 Brian Ashton's unfancied team of underdogs beat France in their own back yard, in the Stade de France, for the first time since 2000. A Josh Lewsey try and nine points from the boot of Jonny Wilkinson gave England a battling 14-9 win.

DID YOU KNOW?
The phrase 'Le Crunch' was borrowed from an advertising slogan for French apples but the first recorded use in this context is lost in the annals of rugby history!

Chris Ashton

In club rugby Chris Ashton has been a try machine. He switched to rugby union from rugby league side Wigan Warriors in 2008/09 joining Northampton Saints. In the 2009/10 season, he was top scorer in the Guinness Premiership and joint leader in the Heineken Cup.

Scoring tries is what Chris Ashton is all about though he is well known for his outstanding support play too. He started his career as a rugby league player at Wigan Warriors. He emerged through their development system, eventually scoring 27 tries in 23 academy matches. So it was no surprise to anyone at the club when he made his Super League debut against Hull in 2005 at the age of 18. The following season he was Wigan's top try-scorer and he was chosen for the England rugby league team in the 2006 Federation Shield.

He signed for Northampton Saints on a three-year contract in the 2007/08 season and added another two years in January 2009. He laid down a marker for his try-hungry style by scoring a maiden try with his first touch of the ball on his debut in a 44-11 victory over London Welsh.

He headed the try-scoring list in the European Challenge Cup in 2008/09 and kept the prolific scoring up the next season. In fact he scored so many tries in 2009/10 he not only topped the charts in English senior club rugby but was an easy choice as Guinness Premiership player of the year having also been joint top try-scorer in the Heineken Cup.

Chris's development in rugby league enabled him to go straight into the England senior squad and he made his debut against France in the RBS 6 Nations 2010. He kept his place for England's summer tour and scored against all three of the tour opponents including his debut senior try against Australia in Sydney.

Former Saints captain and team-mate Bruce Reihana says of Chris: "Chris is extremely outgoing and chirpy. He is capable of becoming a very good player."

CLUB:	Northampton Saints
POSITION:	Wing
BORN:	29.03.1987 l Wigan
HEIGHT:	1.83m (6'0")
WEIGHT:	95kg (14st 13lb)
REPRESENTATIVE HONOURS:	(RL) England U18, England
CAPS:	3
POINTS:	5 – 1T
INTERNATIONAL RECORD:	2010 F, A (1, 2)

Dan Ward-Smith

Dan Ward-Smith should already have his first cap for England but fate cruelly intervened in February 2007. He was lined up to make his debut against Scotland in that year's RBS 6 Nations but sustained a dislocated knee for Bristol in the Guinness Premiership a week before that game. The injury kept him out for 10 months.

Born in New Zealand to English parents, he spent time in the West Country as a youngster on his return to the UK. He then returned down under to study at Massey University where he represented New Zealand Maori Colts. However, a brief visit back to Cornwall coincided with Graham Dawe taking charge of Plymouth Albion. The former England hooker was quick to spot Dan's talent and offered him a contract. He stayed for six seasons and scored a club record 93 league tries. He then moved to Bristol before signing for London Wasps.

WHAT THEY SAY

Bristol captain and Wales lock Gareth Llewellyn says "He is right up there with the best number 8s I have played with or against."

CLUB:	London Wasps
POSITION:	Number 8
BORN:	02.01.1978 I Palmerston North, NZ
HEIGHT:	1.93m (6' 4")
WEIGHT:	115kg (18st 1lb)
REPRESENTATIVE HONOURS:	New Zealand Maori Colts, England A
CAPS:	0
POINTS:	0

Shontayne Hape

Shontayne Hape made his debut for England in the first game of the tour down under in 2010. Although England lost he played well enough to keep his place for the second test in Sydney.

A powerful centre, Shontayne was lured into rugby union by a three year contract with Bath Rugby in 2008-09 after a glittering rugby league career. He qualified for England on residence in December 2009 after playing 14 tests for the Kiwis in the 13-man code.

His first rugby league club was Bradford Bulls for whom he scored 15 tries in his debut season. His centre partnership there with Lesley Vainikolo was one of the most devastating in Super League history. They scored 227 tries between them in five seasons and Shontayne appeared in 3 Grand Finals winning two of them.

He first played rugby under his father's tutelage at Te Atatu Roosters and has become known for his quick reading of the game and his powerful presence on the field.

CLUB:	Bath Rugby
POSITION:	Centre
BORN:	30.01.1981 | Auckland, NZ
HEIGHT:	1.88m (6' 2")
WEIGHT:	102kg (16st 1lb)
REPRESENTATIVE HONOURS:	New Zealand Rugby League
CAPS:	2
POINTS:	0

Courtney Lawes

A towering lock, who can also play in the back row, Courtney Lawes made his full debut for England in the 21-20 victory over Australia in summer 2010. He had appeared as a replacement the test week before to gain his third cap.

Just like his Northampton Saints and England contemporaries, Ben Cohen and Steve Thompson, he started his rugby at Northampton Old Scouts. He was educated at Moulton College and toured Australia with the England Under 18 side in 2007, but missed the 2008 Under 20 6 Nations through injury.

He was one of England's best players at the IRB Junior World Championships in Japan in 2009, a tournament where coach Mark Mapletoft's team came runners up to the junior All Blacks. Courtney impressed so much in Japan that he graduated straight into the England Saxons squad the next month and a year later was in the senior squad.

WHAT THEY SAY

Forwards coach at Northampton Saints, Dorian West says "With the amount of game time he's had and his performances at the IRB tournament in Japan, it is easy to forget he only entered our senior academy three years ago."

CLUB:	Northampton Saints
POSITION:	Lock/Flanker
BORN:	23.02.1989 | Northampton
HEIGHT:	2.01m (6' 7")
WEIGHT:	110kg (17st 4lb)
REPRESENTATIVE HONOURS:	England U18, England U20
CAPS:	4
POINTS:	0

Ben Youngs

Ben Youngs's debut try against Australia in Sydney last summer paved the way for a famous England victory and made international rugby pundits sit up and take notice.

Not that anybody at his club Leicester Tigers would have been surprised. He was the club's youngest ever league player when he appeared against Bristol in April 2007 and in 2008 came off the bench to make an impact on the Guinness Premiership final triumph over Gloucester.

Another of England's top players at the IRB Junior World Championships in Japan in 2009, he quickly graduated to the England Sevens squad for his first appearance at the Hong Kong Sevens.

Educated at Gresham's School in his native Norfolk, Ben joined the England Junior National Academy in 2006 and

back then could play fly half, full back, centre or scrum half.

DID YOU KNOW?

Ben is the son of Nick Youngs, also a scrum half for Leicester, who won six England caps. His brother Tom is a centre-turned-hooker who is currently dually registered by the Tigers and Nottingham.

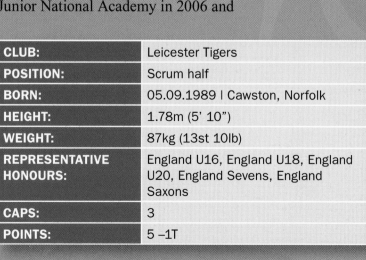

CLUB:	Leicester Tigers
POSITION:	Scrum half
BORN:	05.09.1989 | Cawston, Norfolk
HEIGHT:	1.78m (5' 10")
WEIGHT:	87kg (13st 10lb)
REPRESENTATIVE HONOURS:	England U16, England U18, England U20, England Sevens, England Saxons
CAPS:	3
POINTS:	5 –1T

Dan Cole

Tight-head Dan Cole has made steady progress through the ranks of representative rugby and is now a permanent fixture in the England scrum.

2009/10 was without doubt Dan Cole's best season since turning professional and he is currently Martin Johnson's first choice at tight-head.

The Leicester-born tight-head prop has made steady progress since his school days at Kibworth High School, Robert Smyth and Wyggeston & Queen Elizabeth I College.

He was originally a flanker at South Leicester RFC before signing for Leicester Tigers, where he was immediately loaned to Bedford Blues for the 2006/07 season. He made 16 starts for the Blues and 11 the next season before being recalled to Welford Road for his debut against Bath in the EDF Energy Cup. In 2008/09 he was again loaned out, this time to Nottingham, but upon his recall played 20 games for the Tigers. During his time at Leicester, Dan has enhanced his reputation in the experienced company of England's Julian White, Martin Castrogiovanni of Italy and Argentina's Alex Moreno.

His climb up the ladder of international rugby has been just as sure and steady. His first representative games were for England Under 18s, with whom he won the AER festival in Lille in 2005. He graduated to the Under 19s in 2006 and played every game of the Under 19 6 Nations and IRB World Championships. In the next year he played for England in the Under 20 6 Nations and went on to start all four England Saxons matches in the 2009 Churchill Cup.

His debut for England came in the 2010 RBS 6 Nations match at Twickenham against Wales when he came on as a replacement for David Wilson. He started the next game in Rome against Italy and kept his place for the rest of the tournament and England's tour down under.

CLUB:	Leicester Tigers
POSITION:	Prop
BORN:	09.05.1987 | Leicester
HEIGHT:	1.91m (6' 3")
WEIGHT:	121kg (19st 1lb)
REPRESENTATIVE HONOURS:	England U18, England U19, England U20, England Saxons
CAPS:	7
POINTS:	5 – 1T
INTERNATIONAL RECORD:	2010 W(R), It, I, S, F, A (1, 2)

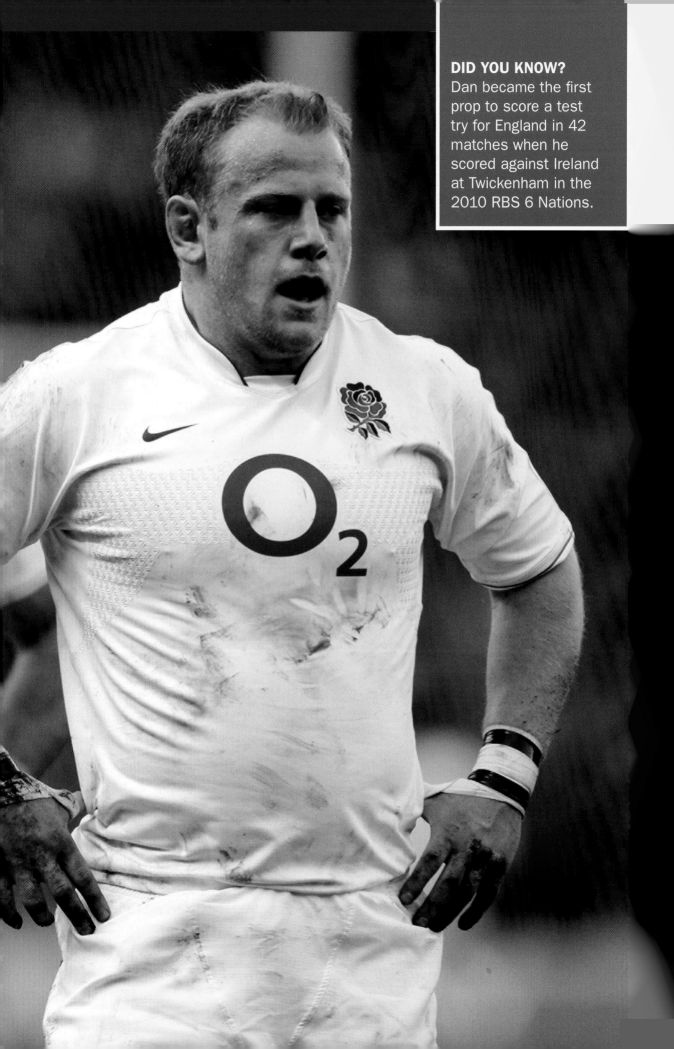

Nick Easter

Number 8 Easter has made himself a regular fixture in England's back row and has missed only ten of the last 44 test matches.

Although a relative latecomer to international rugby Nick Easter has certainly made the most of his chance since his debut in 2007. He has racked up 34 caps and 5 tries since then, including 11 consecutive starts at number 8 in 2008/09.

Other distinctions for England include becoming the first England number 8 to score four tries in a test, against Wales in 2007, and twice captaining his country against the Barbarians at Twickenham.

Educated at Dulwich College and Nottingham Trent University, Nick originally played for Rosslyn Park while working in the City of London. He then moved to Orrell, where he once scored a hat-trick of tries against Northampton Saints in a Powergen Cup game.

He moved back to the capital joining Harlequins in 2003, where he quickly established himself. He was player of the year at The Stoop in 2005 and 2006 and at the end of last season had scored 14 tries in 70 Guinness Premiership games.

Not many players make their full Test debut only eight days after their first appearance for England Saxons but Nick did. He came off the bench to help the Saxons beat Italy A 34-5 at Exeter and then started for England against Italy in a 20-7 victory at Twickenham.

'Mr Consistency' for club and country, Nick also knows where the try line is and is always quick to take an opportunity to attack from scrums or open play.

CLUB:	Harlequins
POSITION:	Number 8
BORN:	15.08.1978 | Leicester
HEIGHT:	1.93m (6' 4")
WEIGHT:	114kg (17st 13lb)
REPRESENTATIVE HONOURS:	England Saxons
CAPS:	34
POINTS:	5 – 1T
INTERNATIONAL RECORD:	2007 It, F, SA, SA, W, F World Cup - SA, Sam, Tg, A, F, SA 2008 It, F, S, I, PI, A, SA, NZ 2009 It, W, I, F, S, Arg (1, 2) 2010 W, It, I, S, F, A (1, 2)

England Under 20s at the IRB Junior World Championship 2010

After coming runners up in their 6 Nations tournament, England Under 20s headed to Argentina for the annual IRB Junior World Championships full of confidence. Coach Mark Mapletoft had taken them to the previous two finals, where they had lost on both occasions to a very strong New Zealand team.

However a third final was too big an ask for a team full of attacking flair. Based in the city of Rosario and playing all their games at the home of local soccer giants Newell's Old Boys, England started well enough. They came from behind to beat the hosts 48-22 in front of a passionate crowd of over 10,000 fans. A hat-trick of tries from Gloucester Rugby's Jonny May was the highlight. London Irish full back Tom Homer also landed the kick that made him the all-time points leader in the IRB Junior World Championships.

England were desperate for revenge against Ireland in the next pool game as the men in green had beaten them in both their previous 6 Nations encounters. Again it was Gloucester and London Irish players who provided the points as replacement Freddie Burns (Gloucester) and Jamie Gibson

(London Irish) scored the tries that gave England a 36-21 victory.

A tense affair in the final pool game saw England beat France 17-9, in a game where Jamie Gibson popped up again to grab the only try. In the semi final against Australia, England's poor tackling afforded a scintillating Wallaby back line too many chances and they lost the game 28-16. Sam Smith of Harlequins and Jonny May scored tries but it wasn't enough.

The 3rd place play-off was a similar affair, England dominated in the scrum and line-out but allowed South Africa too much space, and despite leading at half time with tries from Marcus Watson, Joe Marler and Freddie Burns, they lost 22-27.

IRB JWC 2010 ARGENTINA
Pool B
Argentina 22 England 48
England 36 Ireland 21
England 17 France 9

Semi final
Australia 28 England 16

3rd place play-off
England 22 South Africa 27

England Counties Tour to Canada 2010

England Counties ticked all the boxes on their three-match tour to Canada in 2010. They finished the trip unbeaten and extended their unbeaten record in North America to six matches. More importantly, however, they provided yet another group of players with the chance to wear an England shirt and to develop their skills in a challenging rugby environment.

21 clubs and 13 counties were represented in manager Danny Hodgson's squad where the average age of just 22 points to the development potential for all the players involved.

The first game in St. John's, Newfoundland was played in atrocious conditions of almost horizontal rain and biting cold, so it was to the enormous credit of the Counties players that they retained their composure and managed to register a 20-6 win.

The next game v Ontario Blues in Toronto was played in temperatures at least 20 degrees centigrade warmer but was quite a bit closer with England eventually edging out the locals 32-26.

The final game against British Columbia Bears had been forecast to be the toughest of the trip, but turned out to be the one where the Counties really found their best form, and a 46-7 victory wrapped up the trip and Manager Danny Hodgson's association with the team in fine style.

England Counties Tour of Canada 2010
Newfoundland Rock 6 England Counties XV 20
Ontario Blues 26 England Counties XV 32
British Columbia Bears 7 England Counties XV 46

The England Squad...
Did You Know?

THE THIRD DEGREE

Did you know... that many England players graduated from university, among them are:

- Nick Easter, Nottingham Trent
- Tom Palmer, Leeds
- Charlie Hodgson, Durham
- Paul Doran-Jones, University College, Dublin
- Ben Foden, Manchester
- Joe Simpson, London School of Economics

MORE STRINGS TO MY BOW

Did you know... that many of the England players were successful performers at other sports?

- Olly Barkley had soccer trials for Arsenal and Plymouth Argyle but originally preferred basketball.
- David Strettle had trials for Liverpool and Manchester City.
- Delon Armitage nearly became a footballer with Villeneuve-Loubet as a youngster in France.
- Chris Ashton was already making a big name for himself in rugby league before switching codes.
- Matt Banahan played for both Jersey and the West of England at hockey.

HUMBLE BEGINNINGS

Did you know... that most of the England squad started at smaller clubs (just like you, perhaps!)? Here are some of them:

- Courtney Lawes, Northampton Old Scouts
- Danny Care, Otley
- Chris Robshaw, Warlingham RFC
- Shontayne Hape, Te Atatu Roosters
- Dan Cole, South Leicester RFC
- David Attwood, Dings Crusaders

ONE BORN EVERY MINUTE

These days of course, players can qualify to play international rugby through qualification but...Did you know... some of the England players weren't born in England?

- Delon & Steffon Armitage - San Fernando, Trinidad
- Matt Banahan - St. Brelade, Jersey
- Simon Shaw - Nairobi, Kenya
- Joe Simpson - Sydney, Australia

Tom Palmer

Lock Tom Palmer is something of a rugby globetrotter. Although he was born in London, he plays his club rugby in France and as a young player represented New Zealand Schools and Scotland Under 19s and Under 21s.

Tom Palmer made his debut for England against the USA in San Francisco in June 2001 but despite being a squad regular had to wait nearly 8 years for his second chance. This came against South Africa in the autumn test in 2008, but he sustained a shoulder injury for his club London Wasps, which ruled him out of the 2009 RBS 6 Nations.

He returned to England action again coming on as replacement against France in Paris in the last game of the 2010 RBS 6 Nations and went on to start both games against Australia on the summer tour.

He signed for London Wasps in 2006 after eight seasons with Leeds Carnegie (then known as Leeds Tykes). During that time he became the club's first international player and its youngest ever captain. He played 188 times for them before moving to London with Wasps and then signed for the Parisian club Stade Francais in 2009.

Tom, a shrewd operator and specialist in the line-out, started his rugby as a minis player with Barnet in London and then for Boroughmuir High School in Scotland.

CLUB:	Stade Francais
POSITION:	Lock
BORN:	27.03.1979 I London
HEIGHT:	1.99m (6' 6")
WEIGHT:	113kg (17st 11lb)
REPRESENTATIVE HONOURS:	New Zealand Schools, Scotland U19, Scotland U21, England A, England Saxons
CAPS:	16
POINTS:	0
INTERNATIONAL RECORD:	2001 USA(R) 2006 Arg(R), SA, SA 2007 It(R), I(R), F, W 2008 NZ(1, 2), PI(R), A, SA 2010 F(R), A (1, 2)

Spot the Ball

ANSWERS ON PAGE 61

England Rugby Wordsearch

How good are you at finding hidden words? Find and circle all 20 of the England and rugby-related words we've hidden here in our wordsearch. Remember the words could be written vertically, horizontally, diagonally or even backwards.

H	J	R	N	B	A	C	K	R	O	W	D	J	B	J
T	Y	Y	E	I	R	E	D	R	O	S	E	K	Q	D
P	Y	E	M	T	T	J	G	N	L	V	C	V	T	P
O	N	A	F	C	U	U	F	T	Y	U	K	H	Z	L
S	E	S	J	L	Y	H	P	Y	R	T	F	Y	C	T
T	D	T	E	L	O	C	C	M	O	N	Y	E	V	F
S	O	E	F	L	K	O	F	M	W	A	W	S	N	L
P	F	R	W	E	H	T	D	R	S	W	C	O	L	B
X	Y	K	J	I	K	Y	V	H	O	R	S	E	K	V
V	T	K	J	R	B	Z	T	R	U	N	K	Z	K	X
L	L	K	W	U	M	O	L	M	H	S	T	M	N	R
L	A	F	F	O	N	D	C	O	A	K	G	R	X	L
L	N	F	M	F	C	A	J	H	X	L	W	W	O	T
R	E	L	T	U	P	S	I	L	L	E	B	B	E	W
F	P	N	P	W	R	N	R	H	C	Q	J	L	K	Z

ASHTON	FLOOD	JOHNSON	RED ROSE
BACK ROW	FODEN	MONYE	RUCK
CHUTER	FOURIE	PENALTY	SCRUM CAP
COLE	FRONT ROW	POSTS	WEBB ELLIS
EASTER	HASKELL	PUT IN	WORLD CUP

ANSWERS ON PAGE 61

Rugby World Cup 2011 Preview

New Zealand welcomes the world of rugby.

In September and October 2011 the Rugby World Cup will return to New Zealand, the country where the tournament was first played in 1987. Since then England have played in three of the six finals, including of course the famous win for Clive Woodward's team in Sydney in 2003 and *that* dropped goal by Jonny Wilkinson.

20 teams will play 48 matches in the 2011 tournament at 12 venues across New Zealand. England are second seeds in Pool B and will face Argentina, Scotland, Georgia and the winner of the international play-off system.

The All Blacks will be desperate to win on home soil having not won since the inaugural

RUGBY WORLD CUP 2011

Pool A	Pool B	Pool C	Pool D
New Zealand	Argentina	Australia	South Africa
France	England	Ireland	Wales
Tonga	Scotland	Italy	Fiji
Canada	Georgia	Russia	Samoa
Japan	*Play off winners*	USA	Namibia

tournament. But they are also looking forward to hosting the world of rugby again. CEO of the event, Martin Snedden said "We really want our thousands of international guests to not just soak up and love the rugby but to also enjoy our beautiful country and our friendly people." It is estimated that up to 60,000 fans will visit New Zealand for the event. England will not find it easy in New Zealand, having to get past both Argentina and Scotland in the pool stage, but as they showed at the last Rugby World Cup in France, they are a team that should never be written off!

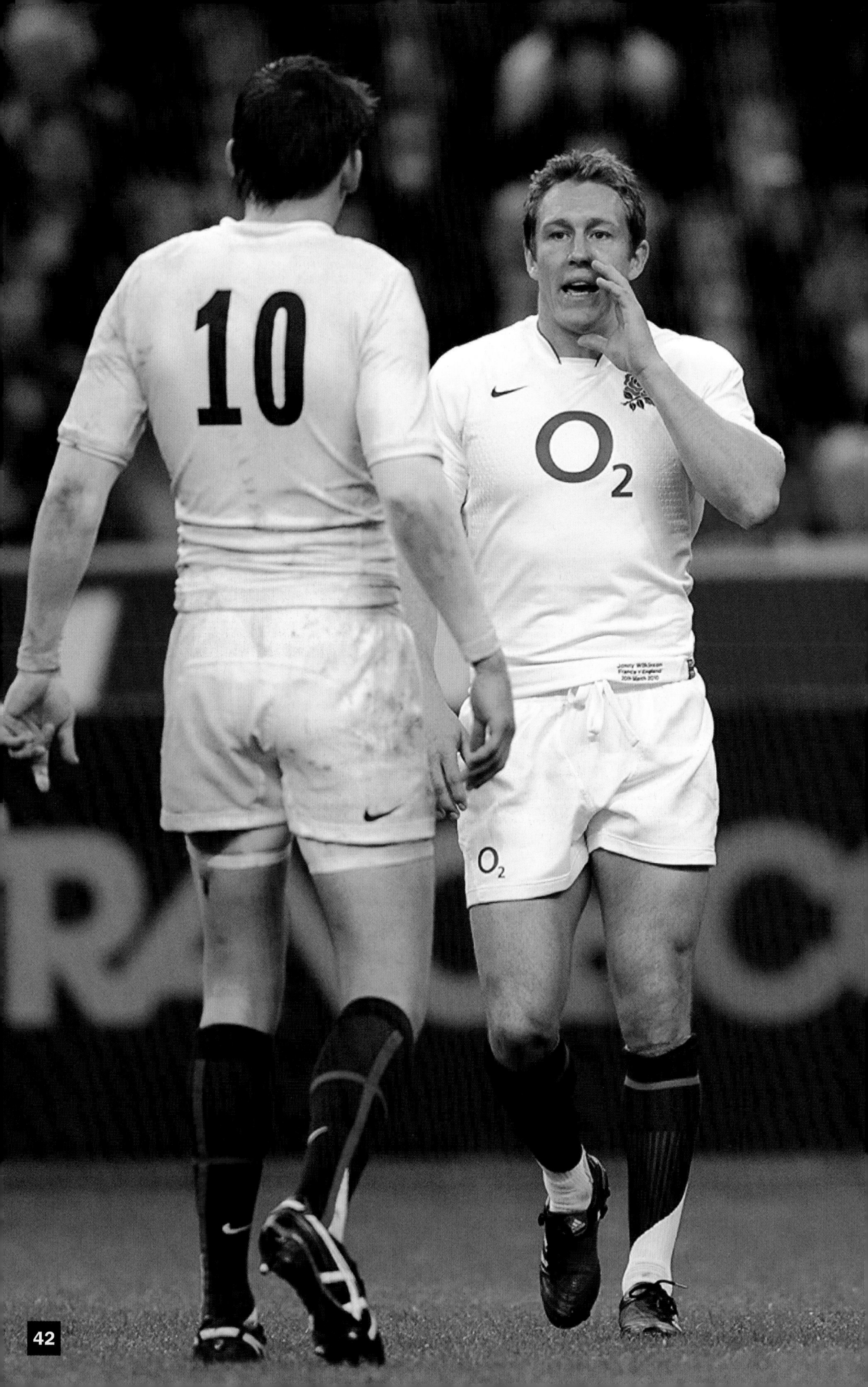
10
O2
O2

Guess Who?

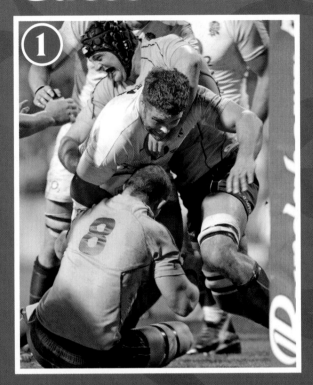

ANSWERS ON PAGE 61

England Saxons Win the 2010 Churchill Cup

England's A team is these days known as England Saxons and gives the senior coaches a great chance to see how young players are developing. Crucially it also gives players who have been on the fringe of the senior squad or even those with caps to keep in the shop window of international rugby.

In 2010 England Saxons won the Churchill Cup for an unprecedented fifth time when they beat Canada in the final. The six match tournament also featured the Russian, Uruguayan and USA national sides as well as France A.

The pool games were played at Infinity Park in Colorado, one of the few rugby-specific venues in the USA. After the pool stages, all six teams headed across the states to the Red Bull Arena in Harrison New Jersey for the finals.

England started their campaign with a 49-17 win over Russia, following that by beating the USA 32-9 which gave them their place in the final against Canada.

Bath Rugby's Nick Abendanon and Saracens' Alex Goode both crossed the try-line as the Saxons raced out into an early 17-0 lead, with Northampton Saints fly half Stephen Myler adding two conversions and a penalty.

Canada, playing in their first Churchill Cup final, responded through tries from Matt Evans and Chauncey O'Toole, but the reliable boot of Myler slotted two more penalties through the posts to give the Saxons a 10-point half-time lead.

The contest was effectively decided when Northampton Saints centre Jon Clarke touched down in the opening stages of the second half. Gloucester Rugby No. 8 Luke Narraway then added another try with 20 minutes left as the Saxons put the result beyond all possible doubt. Ryan Smith scored a late consolation try for Canada but the stylish Saxons were never in danger of letting their lead slip.

Saxons Head Coach Stuart Lancaster was full of praise for his young side: "It's a fantastic achievement," he said. "Three weeks ago we met in a Heathrow hotel with disappointed players not making the senior tour and young players who came in straight from the Premiership, and collectively to put all that together and form a team is great, I'm really proud."

THE CHURCHILL CUP 2010

Pool Games:
Uruguay 6 Canada 48
Russia 22 USA 39
Russia 17 England Saxons 49
Uruguay 10 France A 43
England Saxons 32 USA 9
France A 27 Canada 33

Finals:
Russia 38 Uruguay 19
USA 10 France A 24
England Saxons 38 Canada 18

Mark Cueto

Mark Cueto owes his exotic surname to his Spanish Grandfather but is as English as they come, having been born in Workington and played all his professional rugby at Sale Sharks.

Mark Cueto was the third of only ten players ever to score 50 tries in the Guinness Premiership. A one-club man, he has played all his professional rugby so far for Sale Sharks and has over 40 England caps and fifteen tries under his belt.

He made his debut in 2003 after scoring five tries in ten matches for England A in the same season. This tally included a hat-trick in a 78-6 win over Scotland A at Northampton's Franklin Gardens. He launched his test career with four tries in three games. Although his highlight as an England player could have been a try in a World Cup final but for the 'TMO' (Television Match Official) who ruled his foot was over the line when touching down against South Africa in the 2007 final in Paris. He also has a British & Irish Lions cap and has played for England Universities, Sevens and Saxons.

Mark first played mini rugby at Netherhall, and then joined Altrincham Kersal after 12 years playing soccer. He was educated at Thomas Moore CHS and went on to obtain a BA in Sport Science from Manchester Metropolitan University.

CLUB:	Sale Sharks
POSITION:	Wing
BORN:	26.12.1979	Workington
HEIGHT:	1.83m (6' 0")
WEIGHT:	95kg (14st 13lb)
REPRESENTATIVE HONOURS:	England Universities, England Sevens, England A, England Saxons
CAPS:	41
POINTS:	75 – 15T
INTERNATIONAL RECORD:	England 2004 C, SA, A 2005 W, F, I, It, S, A, NZ, Sam 2006 W, It, S, F, I, SA (1, 2) 2007 W, F World Cup - USA, Sam, Tg, SA 2009 It, W, I, F, S, Arg (1, 2), A, Arg, NZ 2010 W, It, I, S, F, A (1, 2) Lions 2005 NZ (3)

DID YOU KNOW?
In 2005 Mark equalled a record set by Chris Oti in 1991 when he scored tries in eight consecutive Guinness Premiership matches.

England Down Under: Summer Tour Report 2010

From the highs of a superb, battling win against Australia in Sydney to the lows of a defeat to the New Zealand Maori in the last game, England's tour down under in 2010 was a mixed bag.

England needed a late comeback in their opening game to rescue the match against the Australian Barbarians. Teenager James O'Connor justified his selection for the Aussie Baa Baas with a hat-trick of tries and 25 of 28 points. Lee Mears, Dan Ward-Smith and Matt Banahan replied with a try each and Olly Barkley added 13 points with his boot. The match finished 28-28 but the consensus was England had blown the chance to start with a win.

O'Connor was again one of England's tormentors in the first test match three days later at the same venue. The young full back stepped up to the senior side and kicked

9 points as Australia beat England 27-17. First half tries from skipper Rocky Elsom and Quade Cooper gave The Wallabies a 14-0 half-time lead. England's pack totally dominated the second half though and forced two penalty tries. Toby Flood added two conversions and a penalty to give England 17 points but Quade added another try and a penalty to see Australia home 27-17.

England's tour began to pick up with a hard-fought 9-15 victory against the Australian Barbarians in Gosford. Once again dominance in the scrum lay the foundations for the win as two penalties from Charlie Hodgson and three from Olly Barkley won England the game.

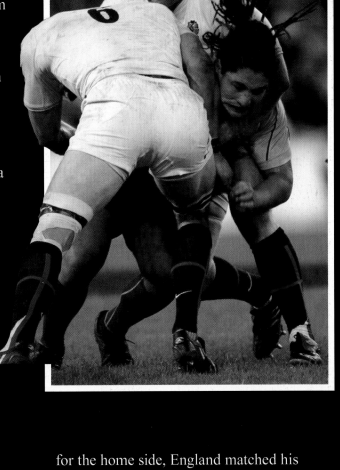

The high point of the tour came in the second test in Sydney. Although Matt Giteau scored a brace of tries and kicked ten points for the home side, England matched his one-man show. Scrum half Ben Youngs and Chris Ashton scored tries in the first half, which Toby Flood added to with 8 kicked points. Replacement Jonny Wilkinson landed a late penalty to win the game.

Before returning home, part of England's touring party made the short trip to Napier in New Zealand. Unfortunately missed chances again put paid to their hopes of a win. Although Steffon Armitage, Danny Care and Chris Ashton scored tries, the Maori won a high scoring game 35-28.

ENGLAND SUMMER TOUR 2010	
June 8	Australia Barbarians 28 England 28
June 12	Australia 27 England 17
June 15	Australia Barbarians 9 England 15
June 19	Australia 20 England 21
June 23	New Zealand Maori 35 England 28

England Sevens

The England Sevens squad tours the world in the annual IRB Sevens World Series, a tournament which excites the crowds with tries galore in a fast-paced, high-octane form of the game.

Under the stewardship of coach Ben Ryan and led by captain Kevin Barrett, the England Sevens squad took two titles in 2009 – in Wellington and London – but found it much tougher going in 2010, as they finished the season 5th in the overall IRB World Series.

The World Series was won for the first time by Samoa who won the tournament in the USA, Hong Kong, Australia and Scotland.

New Zealand won in Dubai and South Africa, while Australia won in London and Fiji captured the title in New Zealand.

England's best showing was at the Hong Kong Sevens, an event where they have been particularly strong in recent years. They finished with 20 points and lost by just 4 points, 28-24 in the Cup semi-final to eventual winners, Samoa.

Arguably England's greatest-ever Sevens player Ben Gollings however had another superb season. He now stands proudly at the top of the all-time player points table for the IRB Sevens with 2,374 points. He is also lying second in the all time player's tries table with 202 tries, behind Argentina's Santiago Gomez Cora who is on 230.

Ben is also the only current player from any country to have been involved with the IRB Sevens Series right from the start in 1999. In an interview on the IRB website this year he said his best memory of the series was "Winning Hong Kong 2006 without doubt. A year after the disappointments of losing the Rugby World Cup Sevens semi there to Fiji, to score the winning try and conversion in the final was as good as it gets."

DELON ARMITAGE

CLUB: London Irish
POSITION: Full Back/centre
BORN: 15.12.1983
BIRTHPLACE: San Fernando, Trinidad
HEIGHT: 1.85m
WEIGHT: 93kg
CAPS: 15
POINTS: 34 – 5T, DG, 2P

CHRIS ASHTON

CLUB: Northampton Saints
POSITION: Wing
BORN: 29.03.1987
BIRTHPLACE: Wigan
HEIGHT: 1.83m
WEIGHT: 95kg
CAPS: 3
POINTS: 5 – 1T

DAVID ATTWOOD

CLUB: Gloucester
POSITION: Lock
BORN: 05.04.1987
BIRTHPLACE: Bristol
HEIGHT: 2.01m
WEIGHT: 115kg
CAPS: 0
POINTS: 0

MATT BANAHAN

CLUB: Bath Rugby
POSITION: Wing
BORN: 30.12.1986
BIRTHPLACE: St. Brelade, Jersey
HEIGHT: 2.01m
WEIGHT: 110kg
CAPS: 5
POINTS: 15 – 3T

DANNY CARE

CLUB: Harlequins
POSITION: Scrum half
BORN: 02.01.1987
BIRTHPLACE: Leeds

HEIGHT: 1.74m
WEIGHT: 84kg
CAPS: 21
POINTS: 13 – 2T, 1 DG

GEORGE CHUTER

CLUB: Leicester Tigers
POSITION: Hooker
BORN: 09.07.1976
BIRTHPLACE: Greenwich

HEIGHT: 1.78m
WEIGHT: 96kg
CAPS: 24
POINTS: 5 – 1T

DAN COLE

CLUB: Leicester Tigers
POSITION: Prop
BORN: 09.05.1987
BIRTHPLACE: Leicester

HEIGHT: 1.91m
WEIGHT: 121kg
CAPS: 7
POINTS: 5 – 1T

TOM CROFT

CLUB: Leicester Tigers
POSITION: Flanker
BORN: 07.11.1985
BIRTHPLACE: Basingstoke

HEIGHT: 1.98m
WEIGHT: 105kg
CAPS: 18
POINTS: 0

ENGLAND SQUAD PROFILES

MARK CUETO

CLUB: Sale Sharks
POSITION: Wing
BORN: 26.12.1979
BIRTHPLACE: Workington

HEIGHT: 1.83m
WEIGHT: 95kg
CAPS: 41
POINTS: 75 – 15T

PAUL DORAN-JONES

CLUB: Gloucester Rugby
POSITION: Prop
BORN: 02.05.1985
BIRTHPLACE: Enfield

HEIGHT: 1.88m
WEIGHT: 116kg
CAPS: 1
POINTS: 0

NICK EASTER

CLUB: Harlequins
POSITION: Number 8
BORN: 15.08.1978
BIRTHPLACE: Epsom

HEIGHT: 1.93m
WEIGHT: 114kg
CAPS: 34
POINTS: 25 – 5T

TOBY FLOOD

CLUB: Leicester Tigers
POSITION: Fly half
BORN: 08.08.1985
BIRTHPLACE: Frimley

HEIGHT: 1.85m
WEIGHT: 95kg
CAPS: 31
POINTS: 83 – 3T, 12C, 15PG, 1DG

RIKI FLUTEY

CLUB: London Wasps
POSITION: Centre
BORN: 10.02.1980
BIRTHPLACE: Wairarapa, New Zealand
HEIGHT: 1.79m
WEIGHT: 93kg
CAPS: 13
POINTS: 20 – 4T

BEN FODEN

CLUB: Northampton Saints
POSITION: Full back
BORN: 22.07.1985
BIRTHPLACE: Chester
HEIGHT: 1.83m
WEIGHT: 93kg
CAPS: 6
POINTS: 5 – 1T

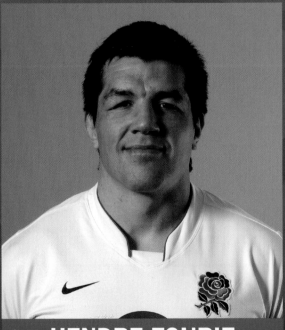

HENDRE FOURIE

CLUB: Leeds Carnegie
POSITION: Back row
BORN: 19.09.1979
BIRTHPLACE: Burgersdorp, South Africa
HEIGHT: 1.83m
WEIGHT: 108kg
CAPS: 0
POINTS: 0

SHONTAYNE HAPE

CLUB: Bath Rugby
POSITION: Centre
BORN: 30.01.1982
BIRTHPLACE: Auckland, New Zealand
HEIGHT: 1.88m
WEIGHT: 102kg
CAPS: 2
POINTS: 0

DYLAN HARTLEY

CLUB: Northampton Saints
POSITION: Hooker
BORN: 24.03.1986
BIRTHPLACE: Rotorua, New Zealand
HEIGHT: 1.85m
WEIGHT: 109kg
CAPS: 19
POINTS: 0

JAMES HASKELL

CLUB: Stade Francais
POSITION: Flanker
BORN: 02.04.1985
BIRTHPLACE: Windsor
HEIGHT: 1.93m
WEIGHT: 114kg
CAPS: 28
POINTS: 10 – 2T

COURTNEY LAWES

CLUB: Northampton Saints
POSITION: Lock/Flanker
BORN: 23.02.1989
BIRTHPLACE: Northampton
HEIGHT: 2.01m
WEIGHT: 110kg
CAPS: 2
POINTS: 0

LEWIS MOODY MBE

CLUB: Bath Rugby
POSITION: Flanker
BORN: 12.06.1978
BIRTHPLACE: Ascot
HEIGHT: 1.93m
WEIGHT: 103kg
CAPS: 63
POINTS: 45 – 9T

TOM PALMER

CLUB: Stade Francais
POSITION: Lock
BORN: 27.03.1979
BIRTHPLACE: London

HEIGHT: 1.99m
WEIGHT: 113kg
CAPS: 16
POINTS: 0

TIM PAYNE

CLUB: London Wasps
POSITION: Prop
BORN: 29.04.1979
BIRTHPLACE: Swindon

HEIGHT: 1.85m
WEIGHT: 119kg
CAPS: 22
POINTS: 0

SIMON SHAW MBE

CLUB: London Wasps
POSITION: Lock
BORN: 01.09.1973
BIRTHPLACE: Nairobi, Kenya

HEIGHT: 2.03m
WEIGHT: 123kg
CAPS: 59
POINTS: 10 – 2T

ANDREW SHERIDAN

CLUB: Sale Sharks
POSITION: Prop
BORN: 01.11.1979
BIRTHPLACE: Bromley

HEIGHT: 1.93m
WEIGHT: 120kg
CAPS: 32
POINTS: 0

DAVID STRETTLE

CLUB: Saracens
POSITION: Wing
BORN: 23.07.1983
BIRTHPLACE: Warrington

HEIGHT: 1.80m
WEIGHT: 86kg
CAPS: 6
POINTS: 5 – 1T

STEVE THOMPSON MBE

CLUB: Leeds Carnegie
POSITION: Hooker
BORN: 17.07.1978
BIRTHPLACE: Hemel Hempstead

HEIGHT: 1.88m
WEIGHT: 119kg
CAPS: 57
POINTS: 15 – 3T

MIKE TINDALL MBE

CLUB: Gloucester Rugby
POSITION: Centre
BORN: 18.10.1978
BIRTHPLACE: Otley

HEIGHT: 1.86m
WEIGHT: 104kg
CAPS: 63
POINTS: 69 – 13T, 2C

DOMINIC WALDOUCK

CLUB: London Wasps
POSITION: Centre
BORN: 26.09.1987
BIRTHPLACE: London

HEIGHT: 1.81m
WEIGHT: 87kg
CAPS: 0
POINTS: 0

JONNY WILKINSON OBE

CLUB: RC Toulon
POSITION: Fly half
BORN: 25.05.1979
BIRTHPLACE: Frimley
HEIGHT: 1.77m
WEIGHT: 88kg
CAPS: 80
POINTS: 1111 – 6T, 149C, 228PG, 33DG

DAVID WILSON

CLUB: Bath Rugby
POSITION: Prop
BORN: 09.04.1985
BIRTHPLACE: South Shields
HEIGHT: 1.85m
WEIGHT: 122kg
CAPS: 11
POINTS: 0

JOE WORSLEY MBE

CLUB: London Wasps
POSITION: Back row
BORN: 14.06.1977
BIRTHPLACE: London
HEIGHT: 1.95m
WEIGHT: 114kg
CAPS: 77
POINTS: 50 – 10T

BEN YOUNGS

CLUB: Leicester Tigers
POSITION: Scrum half
BORN: 05.09.1989
BIRTHPLACE: Cawston
HEIGHT: 1.78m
WEIGHT: 87kg
CAPS: 3
POINTS: 5 – 1T

England Rugby Quiz

(PAGE 16)

1. Leicester Tigers and Saracens
2. Scrum half
3. Paul Grayson
4. France
5. Red
6. False. It was a 134-0 win over Romania
7. Nick Easter
8. The Hong Kong Sevens
9. London Wasps
10. Her Majesty The Queen
11. Stade Francais
12. Armitage
13. South Africa
14. The Churchill Cup
15. Northampton Saints
16. 82,000
17. True
18. George Chuter
19. Graham Rowntree
20. The Webb Ellis Cup

Spot the Difference

(PAGE 15)

Spot the Ball

(PAGE 38)

England Rugby Wordsearch

(PAGE 39)

H	J	R	N	B	A	C	K	R	O	W	D	J	B	J
T	Y	Y	E	I	R	E	D	R	O	S	E	K	Q	D
P	Y	E	M	T	T	J	G	N	L	V	C	V	T	P
O	N	A	F	C	U	U	F	T	Y	U	K	H	Z	L
S	E	S	J	L	Y	H	P	Y	R	T	F	Y	C	T
T	D	T	E	L	O	C	C	M	O	N	Y	E	V	F
S	O	E	F	L	K	O	F	M	W	A	W	S	N	L
P	F	R	W	E	H	T	D	R	S	W	C	O	L	B
X	Y	K	J	I	K	Y	V	H	O	R	S	E	K	V
V	T	K	J	R	B	Z	T	R	U	N	K	Z	K	X
L	L	K	W	U	M	O	L	M	H	S	T	M	N	R
L	A	F	F	O	N	D	C	O	A	K	G	R	X	L
L	N	F	M	F	C	A	J	H	X	L	W	W	O	T
R	E	L	T	U	P	S	I	L	L	E	B	B	E	W
F	P	N	P	W	R	N	R	H	C	Q	J	L	K	Z

Guess Who?

(PAGE 43)

1. Nick Easter
2. David Attwood
3. Matthew Tait & Steve Borthwick